K
TRUTH ABOUT

The
Resurrection

John Ankerberg
& John Weldon

HARVEST HOUSE PUBLISHERS
Eugene, Oregon 97402

Italics in Scripture quotations have been added
by the authors for emphasis only.

Other books by
John Ankerberg and
John Weldon

Contents

Preface

Every year Americans spend billions of dollars gambling on the one in ten million odds they will win the lottery or some other jackpot. Today, gambling for money seems to be an ordinary part of American life. In another sense, gambling is part of existence itself—everything in life carries some degree of risk. For example, there are no guarantees in a job, marriage, health, children—or in the continuation of life itself. Death alone is guaranteed to us.

Perhaps for most secularists life is something like a casino—lots of excitement with small odds on winning in the end (or, to put it philosophically, on finding the real answers to life).

Throughout history, people have wanted to know the meaning of their lives, but most have never found it. Great philosophers and commoners alike have agonized over the answers to the deepest of personal philosophical questions: Is there a God? Who or what is He? Who are we? What is the purpose of existence? Is life an accident of nature? Where did we come from? What happens when we die? Can we be certain of the truth or is everything relative? What are the implications for a life without meaning?

Could it be true that most people are skeptical today for the wrong reasons? What if real evidence exists to frankly answer the profound questions we have cited? And what if little or no gamble is involved? What if this evidence can be checked, evaluated, sifted, critiqued—and yet still stands? Are you interested in examining this evidence? What if many of the greatest minds of history—skeptics and those trained in evaluating evidence alike—have concluded this evidence is unassailable? Can you logically ignore the implications?

It boils down to this: If the resurrection of Jesus Christ from the dead is true, this is the most unique and important event in human history. This would make Jesus Christ absolutely original and unique when compared to every other religious leader in history. Only the truth of the resurrection undergirds comments like the following. One of the world's leading philosophers, editor of *The Encyclopedia Britannica* and architect of *The Great Books of the Western World*, Mortimer Adler, asserts, "I believe Christianity is the only logical, consistent faith in the

4

world."[1] Philosopher and trial attorney John Warwick Montgomery, who holds nine graduate degrees in the field of law, theology, and history, argues, "The evidence for the truth of Christianity overwhelmingly outweighs competing religious claims and secular world views."[2] Alvin Plantinga, widely considered to be the greatest Protestant philosopher of God in the world, recalls, "For nearly my entire life I have been convinced of the *truth* of Christianity."[3] Even the eminent economist and sociologist George F. Guilder, author of *Wealth and Poverty*, states, "Christianity is true and its truth will be discovered anywhere you look very far."[4]

Of course there are also skeptics in the world, but even they sometimes find it difficult to avoid the subject of their need for God. The preeminent, atheistic philosopher of the twentieth century, Jean-Paul Sarte, once stated, "God is silent and that I cannot deny; everything in myself calls for God and that I cannot forget."[5] Yet before he died, this noted atheist confessed to his life-long companion in an interview published in *Harper's*, "In short [I think of myself] as a being that could, it seems, come only from a creator. . . . And when I think of myself I often think rather in this way, for want of being able to think otherwise."[6]

In a world like ours, where the degree of risk is commensurate with that which is waged, no one can afford to ignore the evidence in this booklet. In a universe where heaven and hell are not just remote possibilities but looming probabilities, only the foolish would walk through life without making absolutely certain that the claims of Christianity were false. Why?

In a world where all religions conflict philosophically and/or theologically, if all aren't wrong then only one can be true. Yet, among almost all non-Christian religions in the world, whether one chooses to believe in them or not has little or no personal consequence. In practical terms, in the end, it doesn't really matter if you believe in them or if they are true or false. But with Christianity it matters—and it matters for all eternity.

No other religion on earth offers objective, empirical evidence in support of its claims. No other religion on earth offers a triune God of infinite love who proved His love for mankind by becoming a man and dying for human sin on the cross. No other religion in the world offers eternal life as a free gift. Christianity, like its founder, Jesus Himself, is absolutely original and unique.[7]

Introduction
The Most Profound Issue for All Time

1. Why is the resurrection so important?

The resurrection of Christ is central to either establishing or disproving the Christian religion. Years ago, the great rationalist Dr. Guignebert, professor of History of Christianity at the Sorbonne (one of the most important professorships in all of France) and honorary associate of the Rationalist Press Association of Great Britain, repudiated the idea of Christ's resurrection, along with all miracles. Nevertheless, he stated, "There would have been no Christianity if the *belief* in the resurrection had not been founded and systematized."[1]

In other words, the resurrection is vital because upon the resurrection of Christ the entirety of Christianity and its claim to truth either stands or falls. In this booklet you will have the opportunity to examine the evidence, critique it, and decide for yourself whether biblical Christianity is true—including all that implies.

2. Did Jesus clearly claim He would rise from the dead?

The first fact to establish is that Jesus Christ truly claimed He would rise from the dead. There must be no mistaking His claim, because it is unique in all history. No one else ever made such claims because no sane or rational person would dare do so. Only a small handful of self-deceived men have ever even *suggested* they might actually rise physically from the dead—and their claims were eventually proven false. So no one in human history did what Jesus did. He repeatedly and publicly predicted His death and resurrection, not only giving the specific *manner* of His death, but also the specific *day* of His resurrection. Think about this.

Who else in all human history ever repeatedly announced He would come back from the dead? Who else predicted He would do so on a very specific day—the third day after His death? In the field of comparative religion, this immediately places Christianity in the position of uniqueness.

What if the Pope publicly declared that he would shortly be executed and rise from the dead on the third day? Or if the president of the United States, Ross Perot, Billy Graham, or Donald Trump made the same claim?

What if your mother or father—or son or daughter—made such a claim? Because we know that the possibility of any person rising from the dead is zero, we would immediately know that something had gone wrong and that the person was either deluded or ill. No one ever rationally makes astounding claims which he knows he cannot possibly fulfill.

But Jesus did. On numerous occasions. And He gave specific details.

Early in His ministry, after the cleansing of the temple, He told the Jews in Jerusalem, "Destroy this temple, and in three days I will raise it up" (John 2:19).

Before His Triumphal Entry into Jerusalem, Jesus predicted: "Behold, we are going up to Jerusalem; and the Son of Man will be delivered to the chief priests and scribes, and they will condemn Him to death, and will deliver Him to the Gentiles to mock and scourge and crucify Him, and on the third day He will be raised up" (Matthew 20:18,19).

After Jesus' transfiguration, He again predicted He would be raised from the dead: "The Son of Man is going to be delivered into the hands of men; and they will kill Him, and He will be raised on the third day" (Matthew 17:22,23; see also Mark 9:31).

Even prior to His crucifixion, when the time was becoming short for His claims to either be proven or refuted, He did not waiver. Jesus again emphasized and predicted that on the third day He would rise from the dead: "And He took the twelve aside and said to them, 'Behold, we are going up to Jerusalem, and all things which are written through the prophets about the Son of Man will be accomplished. For He will be delivered to the Gentiles, and will be mocked and mistreated and spit upon, and after they have scourged Him, they will kill Him; and the third day He will rise again'" (Luke 18:31-33; see also Mark 10:34).

Jesus even predicted the specific *day* of His death by crucifixion—on the Jewish Passover: "You know that after two days the Passover is coming, and the Son of Man is to be delivered up for crucifixion" (Matthew 26:2).

Immediately after the Last Supper, when the disciples had gone to the Mount of Olives, Jesus again predicted His resurrection and provided even more startling predictions about the behavior of others: "Then Jesus said to them, 'You will all fall away because of Me this night, for it is written, "I WILL STRIKE DOWN THE SHEPHERD, AND THE SHEEP OF THE FLOCK SHALL BE SCATTERED." But after I have been raised, I will go before you to Galilee'" (Matthew 26:31,32; see also Mark 14:28).

Now consider for a moment what you have just read. On all the above occasions—and more—Jesus predicted that He would die and be raised from the dead. He also gave additional startling claims or predictions:

1. The resurrection from the dead would be performed by Jesus' own power (John 2:19; 10:18).

2. He predicted that He would endure many sufferings before His death (Mark 8:31). He would be mocked, mistreated, spit on, and scourged or whipped (Luke 18:31-33).

3. He predicted that rejection by the Jewish elders and chief priests would be involved (Mark 8:31).

4. He predicted the events would transpire in Jerusalem (Matthew 20:18).

5. He predicted the chief priests and scribes would condemn Him to death but deliver Him to the Romans (Matthew 20:18,19).

6. He predicted He would fulfill *all* the Old Testament prophecies concerning the Messiah's death and resurrection (Luke 18:31).

7. He predicted He would die by crucifixion (Matthew 26:2).

8. The crucifixion would occur on the day of the Passover (Matthew 26:2).

9. He predicted *all* the disciples would fall away, despite the fact they all gave strong emotional protestations to the contrary (Matthew 26:31-35).

10. He predicted, to the exact day, *when* He would return from the dead, "on the third day" (Luke 18:33).

How does a mere man know such things? How could Jesus be so specific? How could He be certain He would not die by natural or accidental death? Or be murdered by someone or killed in a war? How did He know He would die *by* crucifixion *on* the Passover *in* Jerusalem? Why not in one of a dozen different locations or on one of a hundred different days? How did He know every apostle—to the last man—would desert Him? How could Jesus possibly claim He would fulfill *"all things* which are written through the prophets about the Son of Man" (Luke 18:31), or that *in His own power* He would conquer death? (See John 2:19; 10:18.) How could He predict the exact day He would rise—not to mention all the rest? Had He failed on any one of these predictions, He would have been shown to be wrong, and all His incredible claims about Himself—not the least of which is that He was God (John

5:16-18; 10:27-33)—would have proven false. Indeed, claiming to be God leaves one very few options. But Jesus was not wrong even once! No one has ever proven a falsehood or error in the teachings of Jesus.

We think there is only one explanation: Jesus is who He claimed—the divine Savior of the world, God incarnate, the One to whom our allegiance is due. In the material that follows, we will offer logical, historical, legal, and other evidence for this conclusion.

PART 1
The Evidence Surrounding Jesus' Crucifixion

3. How does Jesus' death give evidence for the resurrection?

If it can be established that Jesus did die on the cross and was seen alive after His death by many credible witnesses, no one can logically doubt He was resurrected from the dead. The evidence may be ignored, but it cannot be denied. As difficult as it may be for some people to fathom, no other logical choice exists. The noted philosopher David Hume once remarked, "That a dead man should come to life has never been observed in any age or country." So, if Jesus Christ provided evidence which has convinced over a billion people throughout history that He actually did rise from the dead, it is clearly the most momentous event ever. But before we can examine the resurrection appearances, we must first prove beyond all doubt that Jesus really died on the cross.

That Jesus really died is doubted by no objective observer familiar with the evidence. In his *Ancient Evidence for the Life of Jesus*, Dr. Gary Habermas points out that historical evidence exists for the death of Christ even from non-Christian sources, including Cornelius Tacitus (A.D. 55–120) whom some acknowledge as the greatest historian of ancient Rome; the noted Jewish historian Josephus (A.D. 37–97); the early (Tannaitic) Talmud; and other accounts. "Of all the events in Jesus' life, more ancient sources specifically mention His death than any other single occurrence. Of the thirty-nine ancient sources, twenty-two relate this fact, often with details. Eleven of these sources are non-Christian, which exhibits an incredible amount of interest in this event."[2]

If we examine the details surrounding the crucifixion we can better understand why no one can logically doubt that Jesus really died.

Detail 1: Jesus was crucified publicly according to standard Roman practice which was both severe and chillingly efficient (John 19:18). Condemned criminals were deliberately placed on public display as a warning to others that they must obey Roman law and authority. Thus, the events were very plain and very public: A squad of four Roman executioners put Jesus to death in front of a large crowd.

Detail 2: The soldiers maintained a careful watch below the cross as indicated by their casting lots for Jesus' garments. Matthew mentions "they *kept watch* over him there" (Matthew 27:36 NIV) and that "the centurion and those with him . . . were *guarding* Jesus" (Matthew 27:54). Crucifixions were so horrible that guards were necessary lest family and friends remove the man from the cross and spare his horrible torment. Part of the soldiers' sworn duty was to make certain the condemned prisoners died.

Detail 3: Dozens of Jesus' friends and enemies watched Him as He died upon the cross. Everyone present heard His death cry. (See Mark 15:39-41; John 19:25-30,34.)

Detail 4: The crucifixion occurred on Friday. However, it was against Jewish law for the body of a condemned man to remain on the cross on the Sabbath day (Saturday). Therefore the Jews requested of Pilate that the prisoners' legs be broken which would cause them to suffocate quickly (John 19:31). They could then, according to Jewish custom, be removed from the cross before the Sabbath began at 6 P.M. Friday. Pilate granted the request and the soldiers came and broke the legs of the two men on Jesus' side (John 19:32).

Detail 5: These soldiers, who were from practice accustomed to determining whether a crucified man was dead or alive, immediately recognized that Jesus was dead: "When they saw that He was already dead, they did not break His legs" (John 19:33, cf., verse 36; Numbers 9:12; Psalm 34:20).

Detail 6: Because it was unusual, if not rare, for a man to die by crucifixion this quickly— and to be doubly sure Jesus was dead—emphatic steps were taken. A soldier pierced Jesus' side with a spear "and immediately there came out blood and water" (John 19:34). This is medical confirmation that the sword had pierced Jesus' heart and that Jesus was dead.[3]

Detail 7: Pilate had the centurion *confirm* that Jesus had died. The only basis upon which Pilate could, by law, release the body to Joseph of Arimathea for burial was to verify the death of Jesus: "[He] . . . went boldly to Pilate and asked for Jesus' body. Pilate was surprised to hear that he was already dead. Summoning the centurion, he asked him if Jesus had already died. When he learned from the centurion that it was so, he gave the body to Joseph" (Mark 15:43-45 NIV).

Detail 8: Jesus' death was directly observed by the apostle John who recorded the entire series of events, including the spear thrust and the death cry. John wrote: "And he who has seen has borne witness, and his witness is true; and he knows that he is telling the truth, so that you also may believe" (John 19:35). In other words, John wanted to be absolutely sure that his readers understood Jesus *had* died on the cross. And because Jesus had died, there is simply no way to account for the subsequent resurrection appearances than by the resurrection itself.

Now consider all that Jesus went through in the events surrounding His crucifixion. He underwent six trials,[4] which included horrible beatings and scourging. This alone killed some men. He carried the heavy beam of the cross (or part of it) part of the way to His crucifixion site. He underwent all the unspeakable tortures of the crucifixion itself. He had a Roman sword thrust through His side, piercing His heart. His death was then confirmed by Roman soldiers. It was confirmed again by the centurion to Pilate.

To think Jesus never died is ludicrous.

Consider one description of a typical crucifixion:

> The condemned man was invariably scourged, and men were known to die under that punishment alone, so severe were the wounds inflicted by this cruel cat-o'-nine-tails inset with pieces of metal. It is possible that Jesus suffered this punishment both from the Jewish and from the Roman authorities (Matthew 26:67ff.; John 19:1). Thereafter, he had to carry the *patibulum* of his cross, and was led out under armed guard to die. . . .

> Heart and lungs . . . were put under immense strain by the position of the crucifixion. When the torture was deemed to have gone on long enough, or in order to ensure that the man was dead, the soldiers would perform the *crurifragium*, or breaking of the legs. This meant that the man, if still alive, could no longer hoist himself [in order to breathe] and would soon expire.

> The physical effects of crucifixion were appalling. Of all death it is the most lingering and agonizing. The unnatural position of the body made every movement a pain. The suspension of the whole body on jagged iron nails (one dating from A.D. 50 has recently been

discovered in Jerusalem) driven through the most sensitive nerve centers of the wrists and ankles, insured constant exquisite torture. The wounds of the nails and the weals from the lash soon became inflamed and even gangrenous. The body's position hindered circulation and caused indescribable pain in the chest. A raging thirst set in, brought on by the burning sun. The flies were thick around the victim. The agony of crucifixion was terrible beyond words.[5]

Indeed, survival from crucifixions was unknown; just as today, men simply do not survive the firing squad, electric chair, lethal injection, or gas chamber. Because the law has decreed the prisoner's death, even if a first attempt fails, procedures are repeated until death occurs. But death from crucifixion was just as certain as any modern method of execution; there was no escape. "I know of only one instance in ancient literature which is remotely comparable. Josephus (*Vita*, 75) tells of a time when he saw a number of captives being crucified; and, noticing three of his friends among them, he asked Titus, the Roman commander, for a reprieve. This was granted, and the men were taken down at once. It seems that they had only just been crucified, but despite being given every care by the most expert physicians available, two of the three died. . . . There can be no doubt that Jesus was dead."[6]

Further, those who removed the body and buried it would certainly have noticed any life on Jesus' part. Had He been alive, they certainly would not have proceeded to bury Him; they would have done all in their power to save Him. But the historical accounts agree that Jesus was buried according to Jewish custom, the body wrapped with 75 pounds of spices and linen (John 19:39 NIV).

All four evangelists say the same: Mark says that Jesus died (Mark 15:37). Matthew says Jesus died (Matthew 27:50). Luke says Jesus died (Luke 23:46). John says Jesus died (John 19:30). The fact that "Christ died" is repeated a dozen times in Acts and the epistles.

There is absolutely no doubt that Jesus Christ died on the cross. There is also no doubt He was later seen *alive* by dozens of eyewitnesses in many different locations over a period of 40 days.

4. How does the burial of Christ supply evidence for His resurrection?

The facts surrounding the burial of Christ give further proof that not only was Christ dead, but it would have been absolutely impossible for anyone to take the body. Even if Jesus had somehow survived crucifixion, the burial wrappings alone would have killed him. In John 19:38-42 (NIV), the apostle describes how Joseph of Arimathea and Nicodemus came and removed Jesus' body from the cross and wrapped it in 75 pounds of linen and spices, according to Jewish custom. This meant Jesus' body was literally encased in this material—something like an Egyptian mummy.

Further, the place where Jesus was buried was common knowledge. It had been observed by both Jesus' friends and enemies (Matthew 27:61,66). Once Jesus was entombed, extraordinary procedures were undertaken to make certain that the body could not be moved or stolen. Jesus' enemies were well aware of His prediction that He would resurrect from the dead on the third day. As far as they were concerned, the only manner in which this could come about would be if the disciples were to steal the body. Therefore, they wanted to be absolutely certain that no one could even approach the tomb. Matthew reports what happened:

> The chief priests and the Pharisees gathered together with Pilate, and said, "Sir, we remember that when He was still alive that deceiver said, 'After three days I am to rise again.' Therefore, give orders for the grave to be made secure until the third day, lest the disciples come and steal Him away and say to the people, 'He has risen from the dead,' and the last deception will be worse than the first." Pilate said to them, "You have a guard; go, make it as secure as you know how." And they went and made the grave secure, and along with the guard they set a seal on the stone (27:62-66).

To safeguard their interests, the authorities both requested and secured a Roman guard next to the tomb. They made it as secure as they could, rolling a massive stone in front of the entrance. They placed the official seal connecting the stone and the grave. The stone could *not* be moved without breaking the seal. The Roman seal not only carried the weight of Roman penal authority behind it, but would also indicate any tampering. "The sealing was done in the presence of the Roman guards who were left in charge to protect the stamp of Roman authority and power."[7] These events make it impossible that someone could have stolen the body of Jesus.

First, consider the gravestone, called a *gloal*. These massive stones were used as protection for the deceased against both man and beast. They usually weighed not less than a ton nor more than two tons.[8]

In this case, a two-ton stone was probably selected because of the fear the disciples might attempt to steal the body in order to "fulfill" Jesus' prediction of rising from the dead. The Jews were told to make the tomb as secure as they knew how and they did so. An indication of this can be seen from a phrase written in parentheses in the codex Bezae manuscript currently in the Cambridge library. This phrase, written next to Mark 16:4, states that the stone against the tomb was one "which twenty men could not roll away."[9] The apostle Mark says the stone was extremely large (Mark 16:4).

Second, the presence of the Roman guard was a further guarantee the body could not be stolen. These soldiers, who routinely participated in crucifixions, were not the caliber of men to allow someone to steal the body. Nor would they foolishly risk their own lives by sleeping on the job, as the Jewish leaders bribed them to say (Matthew 28:11-15). Indeed, it was certain death for a Roman sentinel to sleep at his post. George Currie refers to the discipline of the Roman guard noting that, "The punishment for quitting [one's] post was death according to the laws (dion. hal, antiq. rom. viii.79). The most famous discourse on the strictness of camp discipline is that of Polybius (vi.37-38) which indicates that the fear of punishments produced faultless attention to duty, *especially in the night watches.*"[10] Additional ancient testimony indicates that the death penalty was required for desertion, disobedience in wartime, losing or disposing of one's arms, or taking flight when the example would influence others.[11]

Given the penalties each Roman guard knew would be incurred, plus the commanding weaponry each guard carried,[12] plus their extensive military training and expertise, plus their fanatical devotion to the Roman seal—all of these facts and more indicate with certainty no human source could have removed the body. This is precisely why it took nothing less than an angel from heaven to frighten the guards away (Matthew 28:2-4).

This was also probably the first time in Roman history that a Roman guard had been assigned to watch the grave of a publicly crucified "criminal." Guards were not normally posted at the gravesites of condemned prisoners because the condemned did not ordinarily claim they would rise from the dead—nor did their claims so seriously draw the attention of the religious leaders of the day who feared the consequences of a possible conspiracy. So everything humanly possible had been done to make certain the body could not be stolen. Rome simply didn't want any more trouble from the Jews, who were already trouble enough. So the *first* thing the guard would have done is to inspect the tomb and make certain everything was in order—that the body was still there.

But later, those same soldiers reported the tomb they were guarding was now empty (Matthew 28:11)!

5. Why is the empty tomb compelling evidence for Jesus' resurrection?

Remember, everyone saw Jesus die. Everyone knew where He was buried. Many witnesses saw His body placed in the tomb, and later, the great rock rolled across the entrance and the Roman seal and Roman guard placed on duty to secure it.

But what is most relevant is this: No one at all, at any time, at any place, has ever seriously doubted that the tomb was found empty. Every critic, every critical theory, *accepts the fact of the empty tomb.* As Dr. Wilbur Smith comments, "No man has written, pro or con, on the subject of Christ's resurrection, without finding himself compelled to face this problem of Joseph's empty tomb. That the tomb was empty on Sunday morning is recognized by everyone, no matter how radical a critic he may be; however antisupernatural in all his personal convictions, he never dares to say that the body was still resting in the tomb, however he might attempt to explain the fact that the tomb must have been empty."[13]

Most amazing of all, the Jewish authorities themselves never questioned the report of the Roman guards that the tomb was empty (Matthew 28:11-15). They knew that the guards would never have come back with such a story unless they were reporting an indisputable fact. However, because of the seriousness of the situation, it is also likely that the authorities would also have gone to the tomb to personally examine it. Once they saw that the tomb was empty, they knew they had problems. Thus, their only recourse was to bribe the guards to lie about the disciples stealing the body. (Of course, if the guards were *really* asleep, how did they know it was the *disciples* who took the body?)

In light of all this, what do you think Christ's enemies would have done once the apostles proclaimed that the grave was empty and that Christ was resurrected? It is incredible, with the apostles preaching throughout Jerusalem both day and night that Christ had risen from the dead, that His enemies would not have produced the body had they been able to do so.[14] (See Acts 4:1,2,13-21; 5:14-30,42.) Indeed, there is little doubt that the most exhaustive search would have been made to recover the body. But they never could find it. And we know it couldn't have been stolen because of the Roman guard. The body of Jesus was certainly in the tomb when the guard was placed.

Indeed, had *any* doubts existed concerning the empty tomb, reports would certainly have been widely circulated. But there were none. Prominent lawyer J.N.D. Anderson observes:

> It is also noteworthy in this context that all the references to the empty tomb come in the gospels, which were written for Christians who wanted to know the facts. In the public preaching to those who were not yet convinced, as recorded in the Acts of the Apostles, there was an insistent emphasis on the resurrection, but not a single reference to the tomb. For this I can see only one explanation. There was no point in speaking of the empty tomb, for everyone—friend and foe alike—knew that it was empty. The only points worth arguing about were why it was empty, and what its emptiness proved.[15]

In brief, "If Jesus had not arisen, there would have been evidence that he had not. His enemies would have sought and found this evidence, but the apostles went up and down the very city where he had been crucified and proclaimed right to the faces of his slayers that he had been raised, and no one could produce evidence to the contrary."[16]

Further evidence that the empty tomb signifies Jesus' resurrection is supplied by the odd position of the graveclothes which were found in a cocoon-like shape. This explains why, when John first looked into the empty tomb, "He saw and believed" (John 20:8). He believed because he had little choice. A human body cannot be removed from graveclothes having 75 pounds of embalming spices—not without severely disturbing them. Michael Green, who read classics at Oxford and theology at Cambridge, discusses John's account: "No wonder they were convinced and awed. No graverobber would have been able to enact so remarkable a thing. Nor would it have entered his head. He would simply have taken the body, graveclothes and all.[17]

But there is one more proof of the empty tomb. It is human nature to venerate the burial places of unparalleled religious leaders. Throughout the history of mankind, religious pilgrimages are often made to special shrines honoring a dead prophet—especially his burial place. Jews have the grave of Abraham in Hebron. Muslims have their yearly pilgrimage to Mecca to honor Mohammed. Every year Hindus and Buddhists visit the graves of their noted gurus. Look at the graves of John F. Kennedy or even Elvis Presley. But such has never occurred for Jesus, not in the entire history of Christianity. Why? What could explain this exception to the rule? As former skeptic Frank Morrison notes, "Finally, and this to my mind carried conclusive weight, we cannot find in the contemporary records any trace of a tomb or shrine becoming the center of veneration or worship on the ground that it contained the relics of Jesus. This is inconceivable if it was ever seriously stated at the time that Jesus was really buried elsewhere than in the vacant tomb. Rumor would have asserted a hundred suppositious places where the remains really lay, and pilgrimages innumerable would have been made to them."[18]

When Christians go to see Christ's tomb in Israel, everyone knows they go to see an *empty* tomb. What other religious people on earth do this?

In his historical analysis, *The Son Rises*, Dr. William Lane Craig summarizes ten separate lines of evidence for the empty tomb and then shows how all naturalistic theories of the last 2,000 years have failed to explain it. He observes, "As D.H. Van Daalen has pointed out, it is extremely difficult to object to the empty tomb on historical grounds; those who deny it do so on the basis of theological or philosophical assumptions (like the assumption that miracles are impossible). . . . The weight of the evidence [is] solidly in favor of the historical fact that Jesus' tomb was found empty. . . ."[19]

In conclusion, no one can logically hold the slightest doubt that the tomb of Jesus Christ was empty—which occurred in spite of everyone knowing its exact location, in spite of the Roman guard and seal, and in spite of the best attempts of Jesus' enemies to locate the body.

Virtually every theory ever proposed to explain the empty tomb,* other than the resurrection of Christ, is considerably more difficult to believe than the resurrection itself. This indicates that the only possible reason the tomb was empty is what Christians everywhere have maintained for 2,000 years—Christ literally rose physically from the dead.

---

* E.g., the "swoon," "stolen body," "hallucination," "evaporation," "mistaken identity," and "wrong tomb" theories. Almost no historian or biblical critic accept such theories as credible today.

Of course, an empty tomb by itself is only a mystery. Unless Jesus actually appeared physically alive, the empty tomb is ultimately irrelevant.

Part 2
The Resurrection Appearances

6. Why is the testimony of the people who witnessed Jesus' resurrection compelling evidence?

In considering those who were eyewitness to Jesus' resurrection appearances, here are three reasons their testimony offers important evidence.

1) *Many disciples and all of the apostles testified that they were eyewitnesses of Jesus' resurrection.*

The Oxford American Dictionary defines a witness as "a person who gives evidence in court" or "a person who is present at an event in order to testify to the fact that it took place." According to this, a witness is not giving hearsay, he is giving "something that serves as evidence." It is not opinion or conjecture or anything less than evidence personally and carefully attested to by one who saw it. As far as Jesus Christ rising from the dead is concerned, the method required to confirm it is not extraordinary. A dead man who came to life could give the very same evidence of his being alive as any living person could. So the witnesses only need to be able to distinguish a dead man from a living man. How difficult is this? Is there anyone who would doubt their ability to distinguish a living man from a dead one?

In their early preaching, *all* the apostles repeatedly stressed the *eyewitness* nature of the resurrection to both Jew and Gentile, believer and skeptic alike:

> This Jesus God raised up again, to which *we are all witnesses* (Acts 2:32).

> The one whom God raised from the dead, a fact to which *we are witnesses* (Acts 3:15).

> The God of our fathers raised up Jesus, whom you had put to death . . . and *we are witnesses* of these things (Acts 5:30,32).

The apostle John stressed that, "He who *has seen* has borne *witness*, and his witness *is true*" (John 19:35). He also wrote, "This is the disciple who *bears witness* of these things, and wrote these things; and *we know* that his witness *is true*" (John 21:24).

The Apostle Peter emphasizes that, "We did not follow cleverly devised tales when we made known to you the power and coming of our Lord Jesus Christ, but we were *eye-witnesses* of His majesty" (2 Peter 1:16).

To their hearers the apostles repeatedly stressed that the facts of Christ's death and resurrection were known far and wide. "You know what has happened," they said (Acts 10:37 NIV). While on trial, Paul emphasized the empirical nature of the case for Christ's resurrection, stating that he spoke words "of sober truth" and that all of "this has not been done in a corner" (Acts 26:25,26: cf., 2:22).

Writing in his epistles years later, the apostle John continued to emphasize the empirical, eyewitness nature of the case for the resurrection. *He* knew he had seen the risen Jesus and nothing in the 40-year intervening period had changed his mind: "That which was from the beginning, which we have heard, which we *have seen with our eyes, which we have looked at* ["ho *heorakamen* tois ophthalmois hemon ho *estheasametha;* to scrutinize; examine carefully; to behold intelligently; the two verbs express a 'definite investigation by the observer'" (Westcott) [20]] and our hands *have touched*—this we proclaim concerning the Word of life. The life appeared; we have seen it and *testify to it,* and we proclaim to you the eternal life, which was with the Father and has *appeared* to us. We proclaim to you what we have *seen* and *heard* . . ." (1 John 1:1-3 NIV).

The careful historical researcher and physician, the apostle Luke, also stressed that his own reporting came from *eyewitnesses*: "Many have undertaken to draw up an account of the things that have been fulfilled among us, just as they were handed down to us by those who *from the first were eyewitnesses* and servants of the word. Therefore, since I myself have *carefully investigated everything from the beginning,* it seemed good also to me to write an orderly account for you, most excellent Theophilus, so that you may know *the certainty* of the things you have been taught" (Luke 1:1-4 NIV). (The Greek word he uses for "eyewitnesses" in Luke 1:2, *autoptes,* means, "one who beholds for himself.") Referring to Jesus, Luke says, "After his suffering, he showed himself to these men and gave *many convincing proofs* that he was alive.

He appeared to them over a period of forty days and spoke about the kingdom of God" (Acts 1:3 NIV).

In criminal trials today, most juries are convinced on the basis of two eyewitnesses to an event and sometimes by only one. But any modern trial lawyer is simply ecstatic when he has three eyewitnesses; his chances for a conviction rise to 99 percent.[21] For the resurrection we have far *more* than three eyewitnesses. We have such an abundance of eyewitness testimony the chances are excellent that a modern jury would conclude in favor of the resurrection, even though it happened 2,000 ago. (See Question 10.)

2) The disciples followed Jewish law which commanded them to be truthful witnesses.

The fact the apostles constantly appealed to such eyewitness testimony is all the more believable in light of their own unique Jewish heritage. No religion has ever stressed the importance of truth or a truthful testimony more than the Jewish religion.

In the Hebrew Scriptures, God repeatedly warned His people to be truthful; a false witness was to be considered evil and worthy of punishment. Each of the apostles knew beyond doubt that if they were giving false testimony concerning the resurrection of Christ, not only were they guilty of a serious offense for which they might be stoned to death, they were also false witnesses against God Himself, for which they would give account in the next life.

Consider how the commandments of their own law, as given by God, would encourage sober reporting on the part of the apostles: "You shall not bear false witness . . ." (Exodus 20:16); "you shall not bear a false report; do not join your hand with a wicked man to be a malicious witness" (Exodus 23:1); "on the evidence of two witnesses or three witnesses, he who is to die shall be put to death; he shall not be put to death on the evidence of one witness" (Deuteronomy 17:6); "a single witness shall not rise up against a man on account of any iniquity or any sin which he has committed; on the evidence of two or three witnesses a matter shall be confirmed" (Deuteronomy 19:15); "a false witness will not go unpunished, and he who tells lies will not escape . . . he who tells lies will perish" (Proverbs 19:5,9).

All this explains why the apostle Paul emphasized the importance of being certain that Christ was risen from the dead and the severe consequences of a false testimony: "And if Christ has not been raised, then our preaching is vain, your faith also is vain. Moreover we are even found to be *false witnesses of God*, because we witnessed *against God* that he raised Christ, whom *He did not raise* . . ." (1 Corinthians 15:14,15).

3) The apostles faced persecution and eventual martyrdom for giving testimony to Jesus' resurrection.

Consider the often malicious opposition encountered by these eyewitnesses. Would they repeatedly endure persecution, prison, risking their lives, and face death, for what they knew was a lie? Here is a small sampling of what these witnesses went through. "And as they were speaking to the people, the priests and the captain of the temple guard, and the Sadducees, came upon them, *being greatly disturbed* because they were teaching the people and *proclaiming in Jesus the resurrection* from the dead. And they laid hands on them, and *put them in jail* . . ." (Acts 4:1-3).

"After calling the apostles in, they *flogged them* and ordered them to speak no more in the name of Jesus. . . ." (Acts 5:40).

"And Saul was in hearty agreement with putting him [Stephen] *to death.* And on that day a *great persecution* arose against the church in Jerusalem . . . Saul began *ravaging* the church, entering house after house; and *dragging off* men and women, he would put them *in prison*" (Acts 8:1,3).

"Now about that time Herod the king laid hands on some who belonged to the church, in order to mistreat them. And he had James the brother of John *put to death* with a sword. . . . He proceeded to *arrest Peter* also" (Acts 12:1-3).

In spite of all this persecution, imprisonment, and even execution, "every day, in the temple and from house to house, they kept right on teaching and preaching Jesus as the Christ [i.e., the risen Messiah]" (Acts 5:42). These men not only continued to proclaim that they were direct eyewitnesses of the risen Christ but that the very Old Testament prophets ("Of Him all the prophets bear witness" [Acts 10:43, cf., Romans 3:21]) and God Himself (1 John 5:9,10) were also witnesses of the risen Christ.

One reason we can trust this testimony is because all but one of the apostles died for their belief that Jesus Christ had been resurrected—and they faced death by some of the most painful, cruelest methods known to man: James, the brother of Jesus was stoned to death by Ananias the High Priest; Peter, Andrew, Philip, Simon, Bartholomew, and James, the son of Alphaeus, were all crucified; Matthew and James, the son of Zebedee were put to death by the sword; Thaddaeus was killed by arrows, and Thomas died by a spear thrust.[22] Only the apostle John apparently died a natural death.

These men could be harassed, thrown in prison, flogged, beaten, and killed, but they could *not* be made to deny their conviction that Christ rose again.

Anyone who has read texts such as the classic *Foxe's Book of Martyrs* and more recent versions such as *By Their Blood: Christian Martyrs of the 20th Century* (1979) by James and Marti Hefley knows that Christians around the world can be tortured and killed, but they do not deny that Christ is the risen Lord and Savior.

7. How do the extent and nature of the resurrection appearances prove Jesus rose from the dead?

We have already established that Jesus died on the cross. If it is known that a dead person is subsequently seen alive by many credible eyewitnesses, then no other conclusion exists than that such a person has been raised from the dead.

In the Gospels, we find 12 separate appearances of the resurrected Christ between the period of Easter morning and His ascension 40 days later, although there were undoubtedly more. These include Christ being seen by over 500 people at least once, to the apostles several times, and at various times to other disciples as well. As theologian Michael Green observes: "The appearances of Jesus are as well authenticated as anything in antiquity. . . . There can be no rational doubt that they occurred, and that the main reason why Christians became sure of the resurrection in the earliest days was just this. They could say with assurance, 'We have seen the Lord.' They *knew* it was he."[23] Dr. William Lane Craig comments, "Indeed, so strong is the evidence for these appearances that Wolfhart Pannenberg, perhaps the world's greatest living systematic theologian, has rocked modern, skeptical German theology by building his entire theology precisely on the historical evidence for the resurrection of Jesus as supplied in Paul's list of appearances."[24]

These appearances are as follows:

1. To the women as they returned from the tomb after seeing the angel who informed them Christ had risen (Matthew 28:1-10).
2. To Mary Magdalene at the tomb, probably during her second visit to the tomb that morning (John 20:10-18; Mark 16:9).
3. To Peter sometime before the evening of the resurrection day (Luke 24:34; 1 Corinthians 15:5).

4. To Cleopas and another disciple on the road to Emmaus on Easter afternoon (Mark 16:12; Luke 24:13-35).
5. To ten of the apostles (Thomas is absent) and others whose names are not given gathered together at their evening meal on the eve of Easter day (Luke 24:36-40; John 20:19-23; 1 Corinthians 15:5).
6. A week later to all eleven apostles, including doubting Thomas (John 20:26-28).
7. To a number of the disciples fishing at the Sea of Galilee (John 21:1-23).
8. To the apostles on a specific mountain in Galilee (Matthew 28:16-20).
9. To James (1 Corinthians 15:7).
10. To the apostles on the Mount of Olives at Jerusalem just prior to the ascension (Mark 16:19; Luke 24:50-52; Acts 1:3-9).
11. To 500 witnesses all at once (1 Corinthians 15:6).
12. To the apostle Paul (1 Corinthians 15:8; Acts 9:1-9).

There is considerable variety concerning the circumstances, time, place, and individuals to whom Christ appeared. He appeared to women, men, groups, individuals; He appeared by an open lake, on a mountain, on the road, in the upper room with locked doors, in the country, in town, and on a hillside. Jesus did not appear just once to one person or one group of persons at one time, but to individuals and groups at different times and different locations.

In the chart that follows note the physical nature of the resurrection appearances which indicates these were not individual hallucinations or visions but actual physical appearances. Their number, circumstances, and physicality simply do not fit any of the characteristics of visions or mass hallucinations as is commonly reported by individuals who work in this area and who have compared the characteristics of hallucinations and visions with the records of the New Testament.[25]

In fact, *every* appearance mentioned in the Gospels is of a physical, bodily appearance.[27] But we must also note that these were not the only appearances of Christ. After Jesus' appearance to the skeptical Thomas, the apostle John reports that many additional miracles were performed by the resurrected Jesus *in the presence of the disciples*, but that these were not recorded: "Jesus did many other miraculous signs in the presence of his disciples, which are not recorded in this book. But these are written that you may believe that Jesus is the Christ, the Son of God, and that by believing you may have life in his name" (John 20:30,31 NIV).

The Twelve Appearances of Christ

Persons	Saw	Heard	Touched	Other Evidence
Mary (Magdalene; Jn. 20:10-18)	X	X	X	Empty tomb
Mary & Women (Mt. 28:1-10)	X	X	X	Empty tomb
Peter (1 Co. 15:5, cf. Jn. 20:3-9, Lk. 24:34)	X	X*		Empty tomb, graveclothes
John (Jn. 20:2-10)				Empty tomb, graveclothes
Two Disciples (Lk. 24:13-35)	X	X		Ate with Him
Ten Apostles (Lk. 24:36-49; Jn. 20:19-23)	X	X	X**	Death wounds
Eleven Apostles (Jn. 20:24-31)	X	X	X**	Death wounds
Seven Apostles (Jn. 21)	X	X		Ate with Him
All Apostles (Mk. 16:14-18)	X	X		Ate with Him
Five Hundred Brethren (1 Co. 15:6)	X	X*		
James (1 Co. 15:7)	X	X*		
All Apostles (Acts. 1:4-8)	X	X		
Paul (after Ascension; Acts 9:1-9; 1 Co. 15:8)	X	X		

*Implied   **Offered to be touched

Adapted from *The Battle for the Resurrection* (Scripture references added).[26]

Finally, "We ought not to forget that the evidence was published to the world at the very spot *where* and at the very time *when* the event was said to have happened and that no one was able to controvert it. . . . At a moment when it was yet possible to test every incident, to examine every witness, and to expose every trace of fraud, the apostles openly and unhesitatingly proclaimed the fact" of Christ's resurrection.[28]

Consider a parallel case today. Imagine dozens of startled people, all credible witnesses (with skeptics among them), claiming to have seen former President John F. Kennedy alive in a wide variety of circumstances and locations over a period of 40 days. Imagine over 500 devoted political workers, together, claiming to have seen him all at once. Imagine him giving an hour-long personal interview to two former democratic leaders and then having a leisurely dinner with his cabinet. As difficult as it would be for us to imagine that Kennedy had somehow risen from the dead, what else could be concluded?

The simple fact is that every one of these claimed appearances of President Kennedy could be—and would be—checked out. Yet this is exactly the kind of evidence we find for Jesus' appearances. Dr. Tenney comments, "Confronting a learned and hostile hierarchy who had opposed Jesus bitterly during his lifetime, the apostles did not dare to make indefensible assertions. To claim falsely that Jesus had risen from the dead would expose them to ridicule and would invite disaster to their cause. They were too astute to offer to the public baseless legends or wild dreams as the initial proof of their new faith."[29] What the resurrection appearances prove is that not only was Christ risen, but also that He was who He claimed to be—God incarnate. As Dr. Montgomery points out, only two possible interpretations of the resurrection exist: that given by the person raised, or that given by someone else. "Surely, if only Jesus was raised, He is in a far better position (indeed, in the *only* position!) to interpret or explain it."[30] But the resurrection also proves something else—it establishes the truth of the Christian religion against all others since the veracity of the Christian faith and the resurrection are indissolubly linked.

Part 3
Doubters, Conversions, and
Legal Evidence

8. How does the initial skepticism of the apostles supply evidence for the resurrection?

The disciples were initially skeptics. But the resurrection appearances were of such a convincing character that the disciples became transformed men who proceeded to literally transform the world. That Jesus appeared to the disciples as a group *at least five times* was sufficient to cause them to believe. One brief appearance you could doubt—and most people probably would! Seeing a risen man twice would at least make you stop and think, and, one assumes, make you a bit nervous. But seeing Jesus at least five *different* times over an extended period, and each time He operates within the context of normal activities—no doubt could remain! When Jesus had lengthy conversations with the disciples (Luke 24:27; John, ch. 21), eaten physical food with them at the dinner table (John 21:10-14; Luke 24:30-43), accompanied them on a seven-mile walk (Luke 24:13,28,29), and similar things, they couldn't deny it anymore. And neither could anyone faced with such evidence—even in spite of skepticism.

But we must not forget that the disciples *were* skeptics. Thomas wouldn't believe unless he actually placed his hand inside Jesus' wounds: "But he said to them, 'Unless I shall see in His hands the imprint of the nails, and put my finger into the place of the nails, and put my hand into his side, *I will not believe*'" (John 20:25). When Jesus appeared before him and urged Thomas to do exactly this, Thomas actually placed his hand and fingers into Jesus' wounds. At this point, Thomas had no choice. He could only respond to Jesus, "My Lord and My God" (John 20:28). If you had experienced what Thomas did, wouldn't you have said that also? However, some apostles were so doubtful they behaved almost like modern rationalists—people whose biases won't permit them to believe in a miracle even after they have witnessed it. These apostles didn't even believe when they saw Jesus standing there right in front of them: "But *the eleven disciples* proceeded to Galilee, to the mountain which Jesus had designated. And *when they saw Him*, they worshiped Him; but *some were doubtful*" (Matthew 28:16,17).

Consider this. One of those skeptics was Jesus' own brother, James. (Read Mark 3:20,21; 6:3; John 7:3-5.) What would it take to convince you that your very own brother (whom you grew up with for 30 years, whom you had personally seen publicly executed) had now risen from the dead? It would take a lot of evidence. But James was eventually persuaded and wrote the book of James. The only possible explanation for this change is found in 1 Corinthians 15:7: "then He appeared to James."

After Jesus appeared to Mary Magdalene she went and reported to the apostles that He was risen. But "they were mourning and weeping" and would not believe: "And when they heard that He was alive, and had been seen by her, they *refused to believe it*" (Mark 16:11).

After Jesus appeared to the two disciples on the road to Emmaus and walked with them for up to seven miles, they went and reported to the other apostles, but *"they did not believe them either"* (Mark 16:13).

In fact, the apostles were so reluctant to believe that Jesus Himself rebuked them for their unbelief: "Later Jesus appeared to the Eleven as they were eating; he rebuked them for their lack of faith and their *stubborn refusal* to believe those who had seen him after he had risen" (Mark 16:14 NIV).

In another appearance—after the two disciples on the road to Emmaus went to the apostles claiming that the Lord has really risen—even after Jesus Himself "stood in their midst"—they still would not believe:

> But they were startled and frightened and thought that they were seeing a spirit. And He said to them, "Why are you troubled, and why do doubts arise in your hearts? See My hands and My feet, that it is I Myself; *touch Me and see,* for a spirit does not have flesh and bones as you see that I have." [And when He had said this, He showed them His hands and His feet.] And while *they still could not believe it for joy and were marveling,* He said to them, "Have you anything here to eat?" And they gave Him a piece of broiled fish; and He took it and ate it before them (Luke 24:37-43).

In other words, Jesus had to convince the apostles. "And when He had said this, He showed them both His hands and His side. The disciples therefore rejoiced when they saw the Lord" (John 20:20). Let us ask, "What do *you* think it would have taken to convince such skeptics that Christ had risen?" Nothing more or less than it would take today, and this is exactly what was done back then. There comes a point when skepticism itself is forced to retreat.

Certainly nothing can explain these events except the literal resurrection of Jesus Christ. Again, these appearances were so convincing that the apostles testified to Christ's resurrection even to their deaths. How persuasive is this? "So strong an assurance of truth and sincerity accompanies the declarations of a man who truly believes he is then and there dying that the law admits such declarations as testimony even though to do so violates two major rules of the law of evidence: that against 'hearsay' and the prohibition against testimony which has not been subjected to the test of cross-examination."[31] But the apostles were hardly the only skeptics to be converted; history is full of them.

9. What causes zealous skeptics to convert and believe in the resurrection?

Lawyer, theologian, and philosopher Dr. John Warwick Montgomery points out that, "The historic Christian claim differs qualitatively from the claims of all other world religions at the epistemological point: on the issue of testability."[32] In other words, only Christianity stakes its claim to truthfulness based on historical events open to investigation. And only this openness to critical investigation and verification explains the number of conversions of skeptics throughout history.

Evidence is defined in the *Oxford American Dictionary* as: "1. anything that establishes a fact or gives reason for believing something. 2. statements made or objects produced in a law court as proof or to support a case."

Other religions in the world are believed in *despite* the lack of objective evidence for their truth claims. *Only* Christianity can claim credibility because of the evidence *supporting* its truth claims. The truth is that no genuinely historical/objective evidence exists for the foundational religious claims of Hinduism, Buddhism, Islam, or any other religion.[33]

As scientist, Christian apologist, and biblical commentator Dr. Henry Morris observes, "As a matter of fact, the entire subject of evidences is almost exclusively the domain of *Christian* evidences. Other religions depend on subjective experience and blind faith, tradition, and opinion. Christianity stands or falls upon the objective reality of gigantic supernatural events in history and the evidences therefore. This fact in itself is an evidence of its truth."[34]

One of the most interesting evidences for the truth of Christianity and, in particular, the resurrection, is the testimony of former skeptics, many of whom attempted to disprove it.

A devout Pharisee named Saul was born in Tarsus. Here he was exposed to the most advanced philosophical learning of his day. He had great command of the Greek language and considerable expertise in argument and logic. At age 14 he was sent to study under one of the greatest Jewish rabbis of the period, Gamaliel (probably the grandson of Hillel) (Acts 22:3).

As a Hebrew zealot and Pharisee who "was advancing in Judaism beyond many of my contemporaries . . . being more extremely zealous for my ancestral traditions" (Galatians 1:14), Saul was not so much intending to disprove Christianity as he was attempting to destroy it (Galatians 1:13). There is no doubt he was a skeptic of both Jesus and the claims of Christians for the resurrection. He persecuted many Christians to their death, and literally laid waste to the Church: "And I persecuted this Way to the death, binding and putting both men and women into prisons, as also the high priest and all the Council of the elders can testify" (Acts 22:4,5; cf, 8:1,3; 9:1,2,13; 22:19,20; 26:9-11).

But something changed Saul so radically the world has never quite gotten over it. Even the early Christians, after suffering such persecutions at his hand, could not believe his conversion: "And immediately he began to proclaim Jesus in the synagogues, saying, 'He is the Son of God.' And all those hearing him continued to be amazed, and were saying, 'Is this not he who in Jerusalem destroyed those who called on this name, and who had come here for the purpose of bringing them bound before the chief priests?'"(Acts 9:19-23).

Let us ask you, What was it that converted the greatest enemy of the church, Saul of Tarsus, into its greatest defender? It was a direct appearance by no less than the risen Christ Himself—nothing else would have sufficed. In his own words, Paul [Saul] records the experience of meeting the resurrected Christ and how it changed his life forever. He confessed, "Have I not seen Jesus our Lord?" (1 Corinthians 9:1; see also Acts 22:4-21; Galatians 1:11-24; 1 Corinthians 15:1-19).

Yet few people are aware of the impact that this once committed enemy of the church has had upon the world's history because of his experiencing the resurrected Jesus. Paul's three missionary journeys and lifelong evangelism and church-planting helped to change the Roman Empire and even the destiny of Western civilization. Writing in *Chamber's Encyclopedia*, Archibald MacBride, professor at the University of Aberdeen, asserts of Paul: "Besides his achievements . . . the achievements of Alexander and Napoleon pale into insignificance."[35] Yet Saul [Paul] was one of the greatest skeptics in Christian history.

Consider another former skeptic, Athanagoras. He was a second-century scholar, brilliant apologist, and first-head of the eminent School of Alexandria. He originally intended to write against the faith, being "occupied with searching the Scriptures for arguments against Christianity" but was converted instead.[36]

Augustine of Hippo (A.D. 354–430) was raised in a pagan environment. At the age of 12 he was sent by his parents to the advanced schools in Madaura, a center of pagan culture and learning. He later studied and taught rhetoric in Carthage. He mastered the Latin classics, was deeply influenced by Plato, Neoplatonism, and Manicheanism and was for a period a skeptic of religion. But after careful reading of the Bible and hearing the sermons of Bishop Ambrose while in Milan, he was converted to Christian faith and became the greatest father of the Western church. His two most famous works are *Confessions* and the *City of God*; but he also wrote apologetic texts such as *Contra Academicos* (Against the Academics), a critique of the academic skeptics of his day.[37]

The next 14 centuries contain thousands of additional testimonies of converted skeptics.

In the mid-eighteenth century, Lord George Lyttleton (a member of Parliament and Commissioner of the Treasury) and Gilbert West, Esq., went to Oxford. There they were determined to attack the very basis of Christianity. Lyttleton set out to prove that Saul of Tarsus was never really converted to Christianity, and West intended to demonstrate that Jesus never really rose from the dead.

Each had planned to do a painstaking job, taking a year to establish their case. But as they proceeded, they eventually concluded that Christianity was true. Both became Christians.

West eventually wrote *Observations on the History and Evidences of the Resurrection of Jesus Christ* (1747). George Lyttleton wrote a lengthy text titled *The Conversion of St. Paul* (reprint, 1929). Their correspondence back and forth, showing their surprise at the quality of the evidence, can be found in any university microfilm library. West became totally convinced of the truth of the resurrection and Lyttleton of the genuine conversion of Saint Paul on the basis of it. For example, Lyttleton wrote to West in 1761, "Sir, in a late conversation we had together upon the subject of the Christian religion, I told you that besides all the proofs of it which may be drawn from the prophecies of the Old Testament, from the necessary connection it has with the whole system of the Jewish religion, from the miracles of Christ, and from the evidence given of his reflection by all the other apostles, I thought the conversion and apostleship of Saint Paul alone, duly considered, was of itself a demonstration sufficient to prove Christianity a divine revelation."[38]

In our own century, the conversion of skeptics and doubters has continued. In the 1930s a rationalistic English journalist named Frank Morrison attempted to discover the "real" Jesus Christ. He was convinced that Christ's "history rested upon very insecure foundations"—largely because of the influence of the rationalistic higher criticism so prevalent in his day.[39] Further, he was dogmatically opposed to the miraculous elements in the Gospels. But he was, nevertheless, fascinated by the person of Jesus, who was to him "an almost legendary figure of purity and noble manhood."[40]

Morrison decided to take the crucial "last phase" in the life of Christ and "strip it of its overgrowth of primitive beliefs and dogmatic suppositions, and to see this supremely great Person as he really was." "It seemed to me that if I could come at the truth *why* this man died a cruel death at the hands of the Roman Power, how he himself regarded the matter, and especially how he behaved under the test, I should be very near to the true solution of the problem."[41]

But the book Morrison ended up writing was not the one he intended to. He proceeded to write one of the most able defenses of the resurrection of Christ in our time, *Who Moved the Stone?*

Dr. Cyril E.M. Joad, head of the philosophy department at the University of London, once believed that Jesus was only a man. For many years he was an antagonist of Christianity. But near the end of his life he came to believe that the only solution for mankind was "found in the cross of Jesus Christ." He became a zealous disciple.[42]

Giovanni Papine was one of the foremost Italian intellects of his period, an atheist and vocal enemy of the church, and self-appointed debunker of religion. But he became converted to faith in Christ and, in 1921, penned his *Life of Christ*, stunning most of his friends and admirers.[43]

Cambridge scholar C.S. Lewis, a former atheist, was converted to Christianity on the basis of the evidence, according to his text *Surprised by Joy*. He recalls, "I thought I had the

Christians 'placed' and disposed of forever." But, "A young man who wishes to remain a sound atheist cannot be too careful of his reading. There are traps everywhere—'Bibles laid open, millions of surprises,' as Herbert says, 'Fine nets and stratagems.' God is, if I may say it, very unscrupulous."[44]

But C.S. Lewis became a Christian because the evidence was compelling and he could not escape it. Even against his will he was "brought in kicking, struggling, resentful, and darting [my] eyes in every direction for a chance of escape." The God "whom I so earnestly desired not to meet" became His Lord and Savior.[45] His book on Christian evidences, *Mere Christianity*, is considered a classic and has been responsible for converting thousands to the faith, among them the keen legal mind of former skeptic and Watergate figure Charles Colson, author of *Born Again*.

As a pre-law student, Josh McDowell was also a skeptic of Christianity and believed that every Christian had two minds: one was lost while the other was out looking for it! Eventually challenged to intellectually investigate the Christian truth claims and, thinking this a farce, he accepted the challenge and "as a result, I found historical facts and evidence about Jesus Christ that I never knew existed."[46] He eventually wrote a number of important texts in defense of Christianity, among them *Evidence That Demands a Verdict*, *More Evidence that Demands a Verdict*, *More Than a Carpenter*, and *Daniel in the Lion's Den*.

Dr. Gary Habermas was raised a Christian, but he soon questioned his faith. He concluded that while the resurrection could be believed, he personally doubted it and was skeptical that any evidence for it was really convincing. But after critical examination it was the evidence that brought him around, and he concluded the resurrection was an *established* fact of history.[47] He proceeded to write four important books in defense of the resurrection and related issues: *Ancient Evidence for the Life of Jesus*; *The Resurrection of Jesus: A Rational Inquiry*; *The Resurrection of Jesus: An Apologetic*; and *Did Jesus Rise from the Dead?: The Resurrection Debate*.

As a brilliant philosophy student at Cornell University, John Warwick Montgomery was a convinced skeptic when it came to Christianity. But he, too, was challenged to investigate the evidence for Christianity and became converted. He states, "I went to university as a 'garden-variety' 20th century pagan. And as a result of being *forced*, for intellectual integrity's sake, to check out this evidence, I finally came around."[48] He confessed that had it not been for a committed undergraduate student who continued to challenge him to *really* examine the evidence, he would never have believed. He shares, "I thank God that he cared enough to do the reading to become a good apologist because if I hadn't had someone like that I don't know if I would have become a Christian."[49]

Montgomery went on to graduate from Cornell University with distinction in philosophy (Phi Beta Kappa). Then he earned a Ph.D. from the University of Chicago, a second doctorate in theology from the University of Strasborg, France, plus seven additional graduate degrees in theology, law, library science, and other fields. He has written over 125 scholarly journal articles plus 40 books, many of them defending Christian faith against skeptical views. Highly respected, Montgomery has held numerous prestigious appointments and is a founding member of the World Association of Law Professors. There are many individuals with similar backgrounds, temperaments, and philosophical premises as Dr. Montgomery. They simply do not believe in Christianity apart from sufficient evidence.

Among great literary writers, few can match the brilliance of Malcolm Muggeridge. He, too, was once a skeptic of Christianity, but, near the end of his life, became fully convinced of the truth of the resurrection of Christ, and wrote a book acclaimed by critics, *Jesus: The Man Who Lives* (1975). He states: "The coming of Jesus into the world is the most stupendous event in human history . . ."; and, "What is unique about Jesus is that, on the testimony and in the experience of innumerable people, of all sorts and conditions, of all races and nationalities from the simplest and most primitive to the most sophisticated and cultivated, he remains alive." Muggeridge concludes, "That the Resurrection happened . . . seems to be indubitably true," and "Either Jesus never was or he still is . . . with the utmost certainty, I assert *he still is*."[50]

Famous scholar and archaeologist Sir William Ramsey was educated at Oxford and a professor at both Oxford and Cambridge. He received gold medals from Pope Leo XII, the University of Pennsylvania, the Royal Geographical Society, the Royal Scottish Geographical Society, and was knighted in 1906. He was once a skeptic of Christianity and was convinced that the Bible was fraudulent.

> He had spent years deliberately preparing himself for the announced task of heading an exploration expedition into Asia Minor and Palestine, the home of the

Bible, where he would "dig up the evidence" that the Book was the product of ambitious monks, and not the book from heaven it claimed to be. He regarded the weakest spot in the whole New Testament to be the story of Paul's travels. These had never been thoroughly investigated by one on the spot.

Equipped as no other man had been, he went to the home of the Bible. Here he spent 15 years literally "digging for the evidence." Then in 1896 he published a large volume on *Saint Paul the Traveler and the Roman Citizen*.

The book caused a furor of dismay among the skeptics of the world. Its attitude was utterly unexpected, because it was contrary to the announced intention of the author years before . . . for twenty years more, book after book from the same author came from the press, each filled with additional evidence of the exact, minute truthfulness of the whole New Testament as tested by the spade on the spot. The evidence was so overwhelming that many infidels announced their repudiation of their former unbelief and accepted Christianity. And these books have stood the test of time, not one having been refuted, nor have I found even any attempt to refute them.[51]

Ramsey's own archaeological findings convinced him of the reliability of the Bible and the truth of what it taught. In his *The Bearing of Recent Discovery on the Trustworthiness of the New Testament* and other books, he shows why he came to conclude that, for example, "Luke's history is unsurpassed in respect of its trustworthiness," and "Luke is a historian of the first rank. . . . In short, this author should be placed along with the very greatest of historians."[52]

One of the greatest classical scholars of our century, the outstanding authority on Homer, Dr. John A. Scott, professor of Greek at Northwestern University for some 40 years, one time president of the American Philosophical Association as well as president of the Classical Association of the Midwest and South, wrote a book, *We Would See Jesus*, at the age of 70, concluding a lifetime of ripened convictions. He, too, was convinced that Luke was an accurate historian: "Luke was not only a Doctor and historian, but he was one of the world's greatest men of letters. He wrote the clearest and the best Greek written in that century."[53]

Here we have two of the greatest intellects of recent time (Ramsey and Scott), among many that could be cited, vouching for the historical accuracy and integrity of Luke, who wrote not only the Gospel of Luke, but the book of Acts as well. In the latter book he claimed that the resurrection of Christ had been established "by many *convincing* proofs" (Acts 1:3). It is only by means of such "convincing proofs" that skeptics such as Ramsey and Scott could have been converted in the first place. Indeed, the entire *history* of Christianity involves the conversion of skeptics to Christian faith.

Unfortunately, there are also plenty of scholars who have the evidence laid out clearly before them and still do not believe in the resurrection. For example, Michael Grant, a Fellow of Trinity College, Cambridge, professor of Humanity at Edinburgh University, and president and vice chancellor of the Queens University, Belfast, holds doctorates from Cambridge, Dublin, and Belfest, and is the author of numerous books, among them *The Twelve Caesars*, and *The Army of the Caesars*. In his book *Jesus: An Historian's Review of the Gospels*, he fully admits, "But if we apply the same sort of criteria that we would apply to any other ancient literary sources, then the evidence is firm and plausible enough to necessitate the conclusion that the tomb was indeed found empty."[54]

But he does not believe in the resurrection: "Who had taken the body? There is no way of knowing . . . at all events, it was gone."[55] He even admits how the subsequent events of Christian history astonish the historian, "For by conquering the Roman Empire in the fourth century A.D., Christianity had conquered the entire Western World, for century after century that lay ahead. In a triumph that has been hailed by its advocates as miraculous, and must be regarded by historians, too, as one of the *most astonishing phenomena in the history of the world*, the despised, reviled Galilean became the Lord of countless millions of people over the course of the 1900 years and more between his age and ours."[56]

Yet, perhaps, if Dr. Grant had been both a historian *and* a lawyer, he might have better understood the reason for "the most astonishing phenomena in the history of the world."

10. Would the evidence for the resurrection stand cross examination in a modern court of law?

In Acts 1:3, the historian Luke tells us that Jesus Christ was resurrected from the dead by "many infallible proofs" (KJV). The Greek *en pollois tekmariois* is an expression which is defined in the lexicons as "decisive proof" and indicates the strongest type of legal evidence.[57]

Lawyers, of course, are expertly trained to deal in the matter of evidence. Skeptics can, if they wish, maintain that only the weak-minded would believe in the literal, physical resurrection of Christ, but perhaps this only reveals their own weak-mindedness when it comes to taking the evidence at face value.

Lawyers are not weak-minded. Hundreds of lawyers are represented by The National Christian Legal Society, The O.W. Coburn School of Law, The Rutherford Institute, Lawyers Christian Fellowship, Simon Greenleaf University, Regent University School of Law and other Christian law organizations, schools, and societies. Among their number are some of the most respected lawyers in the country, men and women who have graduated from our leading law schools and gone on to prominence in the world of law. The law schools of Cornell, Harvard, Yale, Boston, New York University, University of Southern California, Georgetown, University of Michigan, Northwestern, Hastings College of Law at U.C. Berkeley, Loyola, and many others are all represented.[58]

Among the Board of Reference or distinguished lectureships given at coauthor Dr. Weldon's alma mater, Simon Greenleaf University, we cite Samuel Ericsson, J.D., Harvard Law School, Renatus J. Chytil, formerly a lecturer at Cornell and an expert on Czechoslovakian law, Dr. John W. Brabner-Smith, Dean Emeritus of the International School of Law, Washington, D.C., and Richard Colby, J.D. Yale Law School, with Twentieth Century Fox.[59] All are Christians who accept the resurrection of Christ as a historic fact. In actuality, the truth of the resurrection can be determined by the very reasoning used in law to determine questions of fact. (Indeed, this is also true for the reliability of the New Testament documents.)

So let us proceed with specific examples of noted legal testimony concerning the resurrection.

Lord Darling, a former Lord Chief Justice in England, states: "In its favor as a living truth there exists such overwhelming evidence, positive and negative, factual and circumstantial, that no intelligent jury in the world could fail to bring in a verdict that the resurrection story is true."[60]

John Singleton Copley (Lord Lyndhurst, 1772–1863) is recognized as one of the greatest legal minds in British history. He was solicitor general of the British government, attorney general of Great Britain, three times the high chancellor of England and elected high steward of the University of Cambridge. He states, "I know pretty well what evidence is; and I tell you, such evidence as that for the Resurrection has never broken down yet."[61]

Hugo Grotius was a noted "jurist and scholar whose works are of fundamental importance in international law," according to the *Encyclopedia Britannica*. He wrote Latin elegies at the age of eight and entered Leiden University at 11.[62] Considered "the father of international law," he wrote *The Truth of the Christian Religion* (1627) in which he legally defended the historic fact of the resurrection.

J.N.D. Anderson, in the words of Armand Nicholi of the Harvard Medical School (*Christianity Today*, March 29, 1968), is a scholar of international repute eminently qualified to deal with the subject of evidence. He is one of the world's leading authorities on Muslim law, dean of the Faculty of Law at the University of London, chairman of the Department of Oriental Law at the School of Oriental and African Studies, and director of the Institute of Advanced Legal Studies at the University of London.[63] In Anderson's text, *Christianity: The Witness of History*, he supplies the standard evidences for the resurrection and asks, "How, then, can the fact of the resurrection be denied?"[64] Anderson further emphasizes, "Lastly, it can be asserted with confidence that men and women disbelieve the Easter story not because of the evidence but in spite of it."[65]

Sir Edward Clark, K.C., observes:

> As a lawyer, I have made a prolonged study of the evidences for the events of the first Easter day. To me the evidence is conclusive, and over and over again in the High Court I have secured the verdict on evidence not nearly so compelling. Inference follows on evidence, and a truthful witness is always artless and disdains effect. The gospel evidence for the resurrection is of this class, and as a lawyer I accept it unreservedly as a testimony of truthful men to facts they were able to substantiate.[66]

Irwin H. Linton was a Washington, D.C. lawyer who argued cases before the U.S. Supreme Court. In his *A Lawyer Examines the Bible*, he challenges his fellow lawyers "by every acid test known to the law . . . to examine the case for the Bible just as they would any important matter submitted to their professional attention by a client. . . ."[67] He believes that the evidence for Christianity is overwhelming and that at least "three independent and converging lines of proof," each of which "is conclusive in itself," establish the truth of the Christian faith.[68] Linton observed that "the logical, historical . . . proofs of . . . Christianity are so indisputable that I have found them to arrest the surprised attention of just about every man to whom I have presented them. . . ."[69] He asserts the resurrection "is not only so established that the greatest lawyers have declared it to be the best proved fact of all history, but it is so supported that it is difficult to conceive of any method or line of proof that it lacks which would make [it] more certain."[70] And that, even among lawyers, "he who does not accept wholeheartedly the evangelical, conservative belief in Christ and the Scriptures has never read, has forgotten, or never been able to weigh—and certainly is utterly unable to refute—the irresistible force of the cumulative evidence upon which such faith rests. . . ."[71]

He concluded the claims of Christian faith are so well established by such a variety of independent and converging proofs that "it has been said again and again by great lawyers that they cannot but be regarded as proved under the strictest rules of evidence used in the highest American and English courts."[72]

Simon Greenleaf was the Royall Professor of Law at Harvard and author of the classic three-volume text, *A Treatise on the Law of Evidence* (1842), which, according to Dr. Wilbur Smith "is still considered the greatest single authority on evidence in the entire literature on legal procedure."[73] Greenleaf himself is considered one of the greatest authorities on common-law evidence in Western history. The *London Law Journal* wrote of him in 1874, "It is no mean honor to America that her schools of jurisprudence have produced two of the finest writers and best esteemed legal authorities in this century—the great and good man, Judge Story, and his eminent and worthy associate Professor Greenleaf. Upon the existing law of evidence (by Greenleaf) more light has shown from the New World than from all the lawyers who adorn the courts of Europe."[74]

Further:

> H.W.H. Knotts in the *Dictionary of American Biography* says of him: "To the efforts of Story and Greenleaf is ascribed the rise of the Harvard Law School to its eminent position among the legal schools of the United States." . . .

> Greenleaf concluded that the resurrection of Christ was one of the best supported events in history . . .[75]

In his book *Testimony of the Evangelists Examined by the Rules of Evidence Administered in Courts of Justice*, Greenleaf states:

> All that Christianity asks of men . . . [is] that they would be consistent with themselves; that they would treat its evidences as they treat the evidence of other things; and that they would try and judge its actors and witnesses, as they deal with their fellow men, when testifying to human affairs and actions, in human tribunals. Let the witnesses [to the resurrection] be compared with themselves, with each other, and with surrounding facts and circumstances; and let their testimony be sifted, as if it were given in a court of justice, on the side of the adverse party, the witness being subjected to a rigorous cross-examination. The result, it is confidently believed, will be an undoubting conviction of their integrity, ability and truth.[76]

Lord Caldecote, Lord Chief Justice of England, observed that an "overwhelming case for the Resurrection could be made merely as a matter of strict evidence"[77] and that "His Resurrection has led me as often as I have tried to examine the evidence to believe it as a fact beyond dispute. . . ."[78] (Cf., Thomas Sherlock's *Trial of the Witnesses of the Resurrection of Jesus Christ*, which places the resurrection in a legally argued forum and in the words of lawyer Irwin Linton, "will give anyone so reading it the comfortable assurance that he knows the utmost that can be said against the proof of the central fact of our faith and also how utterly every such attack can be met and answered."[79] At the end of the legal battle one understands why "the jury returned a verdict in favor of the testimony establishing the fact of Christ's resurrection."[80]

But any lawyer familiar with the evidence could do the same today either for himself or a jury. Although admissibility rules vary by state and no lawyer can guarantee the decision of any jury (no matter how persuasive the evidence), an abundance of lawyers will testify today that the resurrection would stand in the vast majority of law courts. The following statements were taken by us in phone conversations with the individuals cited on March 26-28, 1990, or January 10, 1995. John Whitehead is founder of the Rutherford Institute and one of the leading constitutional attorneys in America. He asserts, "The evidence for the Resurrection, if competently presented, would likely be affirmed in a modern law court."

Larry Donahue is an experienced trial attorney in Los Angeles. He has over 20 years of experience with courtroom law trials. He also teaches courses on legal evidence at Simon Greenleaf University in Anaheim, California, as well as a lengthy course subjecting the biblical eyewitnesses to legal cross-examination titled, "The Resurrection on Trial." He states, "I am convinced that in a civil lawsuit in nearly any courtroom today there is more than sufficient admissible direct and circumstantial evidence that a jury could be persuaded to a preponderance burden of proof that the physical, bodily resurrection of Christ did occur."

Richard F. Duncan holds a national reputation as a legal scholar whose area of speciality is constitutional law. He graduated from Cornell Law School (where he wrote for the *Law Review*) and practiced corporate law at White and Case, a major Wall Street law firm. He has spent 11 years teaching at such law schools as Notre Dame and New York University, and is a tenured professor at the University of Nebraska. Mr. Duncan has written briefs at the Supreme Court level and is the author of a standard text on commercial law widely used by attorneys practicing under the Uniform Commercial Code, *The Law in Practice of Secure Transaction* (Law Journal Seminars Press, 1987). He observes, "The resurrection of Jesus Christ, the central fact of world history, withstands rational analysis precisely because the evidence is so persuasive. . . . I am convinced this verdict would stand in nearly any modern court of law."

A. Eric Johnston is currently a member of the law firm of Seier, Johnston, and Trippe in Birmingham, Alabama. He practices in areas including constitutional law, federal statutory law, and litigation in the federal and state courts on trial and appellate levels. He is a member of the American Bar Association, was the 1988 republican nominee for place four on the Alabama Supreme Court, and has been listed as one of the Outstanding Young Men of America and also in *Who's Who in American Law*. He states, "In a civil court, if the evidence were properly presented, I believe this would be sufficient for a jury to find that Christ did rise from the dead."

Donovan Campbell, Jr., is a graduate of Princeton University and the University of Texas (where he was editor of the *Texas Law Review*). He was admitted to the Texas Bar in 1975; the U.S. Tax Court in 1976; the U.S. Court of Claims in 1977; and the U.S. Court of Appeals for the Fifth Circuit in 1978. He has had wide experience in the field of law and litigation. He states, "If the evidence for the Resurrection were competently presented to a normal jury in a civil court of law at the current time, then a verdict establishing the fact of the resurrection should be obtained."

Larry L. Crain, a graduate of Vanderbilt University, a general partner in the law firm of Ames, Southworth, and Crain in Brentwood, Tennessee, a member of the United States Supreme Court Bar, the Federal Bar Association, and the American Trial Lawyers Association, and who has argued before the Supreme Court agrees in principle with the above statements cited.

Wendell R. Byrd is an Atlanta attorney and graduate of Yale Law School. As a student, he was the first ever to exempt the freshman year at Vanderbilt University, where he graduated summa cum laude; he also received Yale's prize for one of the best two student publications. He is a member of the most prestigious legal organization, The American Law Institute, has published in the *Yale Law Journal* and *Harvard Journal of Law and Public Policy* and has argued before the U.S. Supreme Court. He is listed in *Who's Who in the World*, *Who's Who in the South and Southwest*, and *Who's Who Among Emerging Leaders in America*. He asserts: "In a civil trial I believe the evidence is sufficient that a modern jury should bring in a positive verdict that the Resurrection of Christ did happen."

William Burns Lawless, retired justice of the New York Supreme Court and former dean of Notre Dame Law School, asserts, "When Professor Simon Greenleaf of Harvard Law School published his distinguished treatise on the Law of Evidence in 1842, he analyzed the Resurrection accounts in the Gospels. Under the rules of Evidence then he concluded a Court would admit these accounts and consider their contents reliable. In my opinion that conclusion is as valid in 1995 as it was in 1842."

In *Leading Lawyers Look at the Resurrection*, many other examples are given, such as Sir Lionell Luckhoo who is listed in the *Guinness Book of Records* as the world's "most successful lawyer," with 245 successive murder acquittals. He was knighted twice by the queen of England and appointed high commissioner for Guyana. He declares, "I have spent more than forty-two years as a defense trial lawyer appearing in many parts of the world . . . I say unequivocally the evidence for the resurrection of Jesus Christ is so overwhelming that it compels acceptance by proof which leaves absolutely no doubt."[81]

Such citations could be multiplied indefinitely. We have not mentioned the eminent Lord Chancellor Hailsham, the current lord chancellor of England and Wales,[82] or Lord

Diploch,[83] or Joseph J. Darlington, the only lawyer in the nation's capital to whom a public monument has been erected, whom former president and chief justice of the U.S. Supreme Court William Howard Taft said was one of the three or four greatest lawyers in the nation's history.[84] We have not mentioned Sir Matthew Hale, the great lord chancellor under Oliver Cromwell; John Seldon; Sir Robert Anderson, former head of Scotland Yard, knighted by Queen Victoria for his utmost skill in exposing "the mazes of falsehood . . . discovering truth and separating it from error"; Daniel Webster, Lord Erskine or many others.[85] And, as noted, not merely in the field of law— eminent philosophers, historians, scientists, physicians, theologians, and experts in literature and comparative religion can be cited in abundance, proving that the resurrection of Christ must be seriously considered by any thinking person.[86]

For example, societies of Christian believers exist for most scholarly categories—law, science, history, philosophy, literature, and so forth. Collectively they include thousands of members among whom are some of the most erudite minds of our time. Yet all of them believe in the physical resurrection of Christ *because* they find the evidence convincing. For example, among philosophers we could cite Basil Mitchell, for many years the Nolloth Professor of the Christian Religion at Oxford University and author of *The Justification of Religious Belief*; Alvin Plantinga of Notre Dame has taught at Yale, Harvard, UCLA, Boston University, and University of Chicago and been president of the American Philosophical Association and the Society of Christian Philosophers; Richard Swineburn of Oxford University is widely known as one of the premier rational defenders of Christian faith in the twentieth century and is author of *The Coherence of Theism Faith and Reason*. We also could cite Mortimer J. Adler who has held professorships at Columbia University and the University of Chicago, is director of the *Institute for Philosophical Research*, chairman of the board of editors of the *Encyclopedia Britannica*, architect of *The Great Books of the Western World* and its *Syntopicon*, and author of over 50 books including *Ten Philosophical Mistakes* and *How to Think About God*.[87] Hundreds of other distinguished names could also be added from other scholarly disciplines. Again, men of intellectual caliber as this simply do not believe in the resurrection apart from rational, convincing evidence.

11. Is there additional surprising testimony or evidence—and what are the stakes?

Even committed members of different religions will occasionally acknowledge the historical truth of the resurrection of Jesus. For example, noted Jewish theologian Pinchas Lapide is one of only four Jewish New Testament scholars in the world. In *The Resurrection of Jesus: A Jewish Perspective*, he argues that a critical examination of the documentary evidence leads one to conclude in favor of the historical factuality of Jesus' resurrection: "according to my opinion, the resurrection . . . [is] a fact of history. . . ."[88] He also acknowledges, "Without the resurrection of Jesus, after Golgotha, there would not have been any Christianity. . . ."[89]

That a non-Christian—let alone a leading theologian of the Jewish faith who denies Jesus' Messiahship—should accept Christ's resurrection as a historical fact only bears witness to the strength of the evidence for it. If space permitted, we could quote a great deal more examples of great historians, philosophers, and theologians, all with impeccable academic credentials, who have accepted the resurrection.

In light of all this, how important is it for an individual to *personally* examine the evidence for the resurrection? Consider an illustration involving a professional race-car driver. Suppose that one day, the manufacturer of a precision-crafted automobile came to the track. Now this was no ordinary day, but the day of the Indianapolis 500, one of the greatest days in racing. What if the manufacturer told the driver of his car that, unless the car was carefully checked and repaired, by the tenth lap there was a 50/50 chance the vehicle would explode, killing the driver and perhaps others.

Would this driver laugh at such a warning? Would he really ignore the very manufacturer of his own vehicle and proceed haphazardly with the race? We all know that he wouldn't for one good reason: The manufacturer has credibility—more than enough credibility to warrant investigation of the car. When our life is at stake, all of us listen carefully to credible sources.

But the modern skeptic who doubts the resurrection on mere *a priori* grounds, his own philosophical assumptions, is making a decision equivalent to driving the race car and ignoring a credible source of information. For Christianity, both God and history are the manufacturer (Acts 17:30,31). For Christianity, the credibility of the resurrection is established by historical facts and the one who ignores them or refuses even to examine them places his eternal life in jeopardy. Indeed, the more severe the consequences, the less one should gamble; if Christianity had only a one in a hundred chance of being true, no one should hazard it. After all, how clear must the evidence be before one ceases to risk one's eternal future?

If we all would acknowledge that the race-car driver who rejects the manufacturer's warning is a fool, then what can be said about the individual who refuses to examine credible evidence for the resurrection, and thus risking his own soul and those of others he may mislead?

Michael Murphy correctly observes, *"We ourselves—and not merely the truth claims—are at stake in the investigation."*[97]

Indeed, we ourselves *are* at stake. And the stakes are high because rejection of the resurrected Christ is the ultimate personal tragedy. If the resurrection of Christ balances the scales of both heaven and hell, it would be a terrible waste to eventually be wrong about what so many great minds of history acknowledge as an indisputable fact.

Conclusion: Why It Matters

Now that you have finished reading, what do you intend to do with what you have learned? If Christ did not rise from the dead, then Christianity is a deception and you can forget all about it. But if Christ did rise from the dead, then He is who He claimed to be—God Incarnate (John 1:1; 5:16-18; 8:58; 10:30; 14:6-9).

Surely then, it is our duty to follow Him. He·is the One who is indeed "the Savior of the world" (John 4:42), who atoned for our sins on the cross:

> And He Himself is the propitiation for our sins; and not for ours only, but also for those of the whole world . . . (1 John 2:2; see also John 3:16).

> Jesus said ". . . I am the resurrection and the life; he who believes in Me shall live even if he dies . . ." (John 11:25).

> If we receive the witness of men, the witness of God is greater; for the witness of God is this, that He has borne witness concerning His Son. The one who believes in the Son of God has the witness in Himself; the one who does not believe God has made Him a liar, because he has not believed in the witness that God has borne concerning

His Son. And the witness is this, that God has given us eternal life, and this life is in His Son. He who has the Son has the life; he who does not have the Son of God does not have the life. These things I have written to you who believe in the name of the Son of God, in order that you may know that you have eternal life (1 John 5:9-13).

Our eternal destiny depends on whether or not we believe in Jesus Christ as our personal Savior. (See Matthew 20:28; 25:46; 26:28; John 3:16-18,36; 5:24.) Jesus Himself emphasized, "I told you that you would die in your sins; if you do not believe that I am, you will indeed die in your sins" (John 8:24 NIV).

The Bible teaches that, "All have sinned and fall short of the glory of God," and "the wages of sin is death, but the free gift of God is eternal life in Christ Jesus our Lord" (Romans 3:23; 6:23). Because we have sinned and broken God's laws, we need His forgiveness before we can enter into a personal relationship with Him and inherit eternal life. This gift is *free*. Anyone who wishes can receive Christ as their personal Savior by praying the following prayer. (The exact words are not important, but you may wish to use this as a guide.)

> Dear God, I now turn from my sins. I ask Jesus Christ to enter my life and be my Lord and Savior. I realize that this is a serious decision and commitment, and I do not enter into it lightly. I believe that on the cross Jesus Christ died for my sins, then rose from the dead three days later. I now receive Him into my life as my Lord and Savior. Help me to live a life that is pleasing to You. Amen.

Accepting Christ is a serious commitment. If you have prayed this prayer we encourage you to write us at "The John Ankerberg Show" for help in growing as a Christian. We suggest the following: Begin to read a modern, easy-to-read translation of the Bible (such as the New International or New American Standard Version). Start with the New Testament, Psalms, and Proverbs, then proceed to the rest of the Scriptures. Also, find a church where people honor the Bible as God's Word and Christ as Lord and Savior. Tell someone of your decision to follow Christ and begin to grow in your new relationship with God by talking to Him daily in prayer.

Notes

Preface

1. As cited in an interview in *Christianity Today*, November 19, 1990, p. 34.
2. John Warwick Montgomery, ed., *Evidence for Faith: Deciding the God Question* (Dallas: Word Books, 1991), preface, p. 9.
3. Alvin Plantinga, "A Christian Life Partly Lived," in Kelly James-Clark, ed., *Philosophers Who Believe* (Downers Grove, IL: InterVarsity Press, 1993), p. 69.
4. L. Neff, "Christianity Today Talks to George Guilder," *Christianity Today*, March 6, 1987, p. 35, from David Noebel, *Understanding the Times* (Eugene, OR: Harvest House Publishers, 1991), p. 13.
5. In Clark H. Pinnock, "Cultural Apologetics: An Evangelical Standpoint," *Bibliotheca Sacra*, Jan.-Mar. 1970, p. 61, citing Charles L. Glicksberg, *Literature and Religion*, p. 221.
6. Simone de Beauvoir, "The Existential Death of Jean-Paul Sarte—An Intimate Memoir," *Harpers*, February 1984, p. 39.
7. Cf., Francis Schaeffer, *He Is There and He Is Not Silent* (Wheaton, IL: Tyndale House Publishers, 1972).

Introduction

1. In Wilbur M. Smith, *The Supernaturalness of Christ* (Grand Rapids, MI: Baker Book House, 1974), rpt., p. 190, emphasis added, citing Guignebert, *Jesus* (New York, 1935), p. 536.

Part 1

2. Gary Habermas, *Ancient Evidence for the Life of Jesus: Historical Records of His Death and Resurrection* (New York: Nelson, 1984), pp. 169-70; cf., 87-98.
3. Pierre Barbet, M.D., *A Doctor at Calvary* (Garden City, NY: Doubleday, 1963); E. Symes Thompson, M.D., *On the Physical Cause of the Death of Christ*.
4. Clifford Wilson, *The Trials of Jesus Christ* (Melbourne, Australia: Pacific College of Graduate Studies, 1986).
5. Michael Green, *The Empty Cross of Jesus* (Downers Grove, IL: InterVarsity Press, 1984), pp. 22-23; cf. Thompson.
6. Green, *The Empty Cross of Jesus*, p. 93.
7. Josh McDowell, *Evidence that Demands a Verdict* rev. ed. (San Bernardino, CA: Here's Life Publishers, 1979), p. 7.
8. Merrill Tenney, *The Reality of the Resurrection* (Chicago: Moody Press, 1972), p. 110; cf., McDowell, *Evidence*, p. 208.
9. McDowell, *Evidence*, p. 216.
10. Ibid., p. 212-13, emphasis added.
11. Ibid., p. 213.
12. Ibid., p. 214.
13. Wilbur M. Smith, *Therefore Stand: Christian Apologetics* (Grand Rapids, MI: Baker Book House, 1972), pp. 373-74.
14. Josh McDowell, *More Than a Carpenter* (Wheaton, IL: Tyndale/Living Books, 1983), pp. 91-92.
15. J.N.D. Anderson, *Christianity: The Witness of History* (London: Tyndale Press, 1970), p. 96.
16. R.A. Torrey, "The Certainty and Importance of the Bodily Resurrection of Jesus Christ from the Dead," in Charles L. Feinberg, ed., *The Fundamentals* (Grand Rapids, MI: Kregel Publications, 1964), p. 274.
17. Green, *The Empty Cross of Jesus*, p. 98.
18. Frank Morison, *Who Moved the Stone?* (Downer's Grove, IL: InterVarsity Press, 1969), p. 94.

Part 2

19. William Lane Craig, *The Son Rises: Historical Evidence for the Resurrection of Jesus* (Chicago: Moody Press, 1981), p. 84.
20. In John R.W. Stott, *The Epistles of John*, Tyndale New Testament Commentaries (Grand Rapids, MI: Eerdmans, 1977), p. 60.
21. Personal conversation with Los Angeles Assistant District Attorney Larry Donahue, March 1990.
22. McDowell, *More Than a Carpenter*, p. 61.
23. Green, *The Empty Cross of Jesus*, p. 97.

24. Craig, *The Son Rises*, p. 125.

25. E.g., Leland E. Hinsie, M.D., Robert Jean Cambell, M.D., *Psychiatric Dictionary*, ed. (New York: Oxford University Press, 1970), pp. 333-36, cf., Green, *The Empty Cross of Jesus*, pp. 118-19; W.J. Sparrow-Simpson, *The Resurrection in Modern Thought* (London, 1911), pp. 389-90; Smith, *Therefore Stand*, p. 365; Craig, *The Son Rises*, p. 117.

26. Norman L. Geisler, *The Battle for the Resurrection* (Nashville: Thomas Nelson, 1984), p. 141.

27. Craig, *The Son Rises*, pp. 116-17.

28. Smith, *The Supernaturalness of Christ*, p. 199.

29. Tenney, *Reality*, pp. 123-24.

30. John Warwick Montgomery, "The Jury Returns: A Juridical Defense of Christianity," in John Warwick Montgomery, ed., *Evidence for Faith: Deciding the God Question* (Dallas: Probe/Word, 1991), p. 336.

Part 3

31. Irwin H. Linton, *A Lawyer Examines the Bible: A Defense of the Christian Faith* (San Diego: Creation Life Publishers, 1977), p. 192.

32. Montgomery, "The Jury Returns," p. 319.

33. E.g., cf., John Warwick Montgomery, "How Muslims Do Apologetics," in *Faith Founded on Fact* (New York: Nelson, 1978); David Johnson, *A Reasoned Look at Asian Religions* (Minneapolis: Bethany, 1985); Stuart C. Hackett, *Oriental Philosophy* (Madison, WI: University of Wisconsin Press, 1979); John Weldon, *Buddhism*, M.A. thesis, on file at Simon Greenleaf University, Anaheim, CA.

34. Henry Morris, *Many Infallible Proofs* (San Diego: Master Books, 1982), p. 1.

35. McDowell, *More Than a Carpenter*, p. 86, citing *Chamber's Encyclopedia* (London: Pergamon Press 1966), vol. 10, p. 516.

36. A. Harnack, "Alexandria, School of," *The New Schaff-Herzog Encyclopedia of Religious Knowledge*, vol. 1 (Grand Rapids, MI: Baker Book House, 1977), pp. 124-25, 347, and L. Russ Bush, ed, *Classical Readings in Christian Apologetics: A.D. 100–1800* (Grand Rapids, MI: Zondervan, 1983), p. 31.

37. Bush, *Classical Readings*, pp. 195-98.

38. American Antiquarian Society, *Early American Imprints*, no. 8909 (1639–1800 A.D.), p. 3.

39. Morison, *Who Moved the Stone?* pp. 9-10.

40. Ibid., p. 10.

41. Ibid., p. 11.

42. In McDowell, *Evidence*, p. 351.

43. Ibid., p. 368.

44. C.S. Lewis, *Surprised by Joy* (New York: Harcourt, Brace & World, Inc., 1955), pp. 175, 191.

45. Ibid., pp. 228-29.

46. McDowell, *Evidence*, p. 373.

47. Personal conversations, March 26-28, 1990.

48. "The John Ankerberg Show," transcript of a debate between Dr. John Warwick Montgomery and John K. Naland, televised April 1990, p. 39.

49. John Warwick Montgomery, "Introduction to Apologetics" class notes, *Simon Greenleaf School of Law*, Anaheim, CA, January 1986.

50. Malcolm Muggeridge, *Jesus: The Man Who Lives* (New York: Harper & Row, 1978), pp. 7, 184, 191, emphasis added.

51. In McDowell, *Evidence*, p. 366.

52. William M. Ramsey, *The Bearing of Recent Discovery on the Trustworthiness of the New Testament* (Grand Rapids, MI: Baker Book House, 1959), p. 81; cf. *Luke the Physician*, pp. 177-79, 222.

53. In W.J. Sparrow-Simpson, *The Resurrection in Modern Thought* (London, 1911), p. 405, from Smith, *Therefore Stand*, p. 365.

54. Michael Grant, *Jesus: An Historian's Review of the Gospels* (New York: Charles Schribner's Sons, 1977), p. 176.

55. Ibid.

56. Ibid., pp. 190-91, emphasis added.

57. Joseph Thayer, *Thayer's Greek English Lexicon of the New Testament* (Grand Rapids, MI: Baker Book House, 1982), p. 617; James Hope Moulton, George Milligan, *The Vocabulary of the Greek Testament Illustrated from the Papyri and Other Non-Literary Sources* (Grand Rapids, MI: Eerdmans, 1980), p. 628; Spiros Zodhiates, *The Hebrew-Greek Key Study Bible* (Grand Rapids, MI: Baker Book House, 1985), p. 71; Kurt Aland, et al., *The Greek New Testament* (New York: American Bible Society, 1968), p. 179.

48

58. See the Simon Greenleaf School of Law catalogues, 1989–1990 and future issues.

59. Ibid.

60. In Michael Green, *Man Alive!* (Chicago: InterVarsity Christian Fellowship, 1969), p. 54.

61. In Smith, *Therefore Stand*, p. 425; cf., p. 584.

62. Q.v., "Hugo Grotius," *Encyclopedia Britannica Micropaedia*, vol. 4, p. 753, and references.

63. In McDowell, *Evidence*, pp. 201-02.

64. Anderson, *Christianity: The Witness of History*, p. 90.

65. Ibid., p. 105.

66. In John Stott, *Basic Christianity* (London: InterVarsity Fellowship, 1969), p. 47.

67. Linton, *Lawyer Examines the Bible*, pp. 13, 196.

68. Ibid., p. 192.

69. Ibid., p. 120.

70. Ibid., p. 50.

71. Ibid., p. 45, cf., pp. 16-17.

72. Ibid., p. 16.

73. Smith, *Therefore Stand*, p. 423.

74. Linton, *Lawyer Examines the Bible*, p. 36.

75. In McDowell, *More Than a Carpenter*, p. 97.

76. In John Warwick Montgomery, *The Law Above the Law* (Minneapolis: Bethany House Publishers, 1975), pp. 132-33. (Greenleaf's *Testimony of the Evangelists* is reprinted as an appendix.)

77. In Linton, *Lawyer Examines the Bible*, p. XXIV.

78. Ibid., p. XXV.

79. Ibid., p. 242; Sherlock's text is reproduced herein.

80. Ibid., p. 277.

81. Sir Lionell Luckhoo, *What Is Your Verdict?* (Fellowship Press, 1984), p. 12, cited in Ross Clifford, *Leading Lawyers Look at the Resurrection* (Claremont, CA: Albatross, 1991), p. 112.

82. Lord Chancellor Hailsham, "The Door Wherein I Went" ("On His Conversion and the Truth of Christian Faith"), *The Simon Greenleaf Law Review*, vol. 4; Lord Diplock, ibid., vol. 5, pp. 213-16, the Simon Greenleaf School of Law, Anaheim, CA.

83. Thomas Sherlock, *The Trial of the Witnesses of the Resurrection of Jesus* (rpt.) in John Warwick Montgomery, *Jurisprudence: A Book of Readings*, 1974; also in Linton, *Lawyer Looks at the Bible*.

84. Linton, *Lawyer Looks at the Bible*, p. 186.

85. See Ibid., pp. 14-20, and Stephen D. Williams, *The Bible in Court: A Brief for the Plaintiff* (1925); Judge Clarence Bartlett, *As a Lawyer Sees Jesus: A Logical Analysis of the Scriptural and Historical Record* (Cincinnati, OH: New Life/Standard Publishing, 1960), pp. 127-28; William Webster, "The Credibility of the Resurrection of Christ Upon the Testimony of the Apostles" (1735), *The Simon Greenleaf Law Review* (Anaheim, CA), vol. 6 (1986–1987), pp. 99-145.

86. Cf., the membership of: The Victoria Institute of Great Britain, Christian Medical Society, Creation Research Society, American Scientific Affiliation, Christian Philosophical Society, Evangelical Theological Society, and related professional organizations.

87. See their essays in Kelly James Clark ed., *Philosophers Who Believe: The Spiritual Journeys of Eleven Leading Thinkers* (Downer's Grove, IL: InterVarsity Press, 1993).

88. Pinchas Lapide, *The Resurrection of Jesus: A Jewish Perspective* (Minneapolis: Augsburg Press, 1983), p. 92.

89. Ibid., p. 149; cf., "The John Ankerberg Show," "Do the Messianic Prophecies of the Old Testament Point to Jesus or Someone Else?" program transcript of a debate between Dr. Walter Kaiser and Pinchas Lapide, 1985, p. 32.

90. Brooks Foss Westcott, *The Gospel of the Resurrection*, 4th ed. (London, 1879), p. 46; cf. pp. 4-6.

91. In McDowell, *Evidence* (1972 ed.), p. 200, citing *Journal of Christian Philosophy*, vol. 3, 1884, p. 305.

92. Benjamin B. Warfield, *Selected Shorter Writings*, vol. 1 (John E. Meeter, ed.) (Phillipsburg, NJ: Presbyterian & Reformed, 1980), p. 191.

93. Ibid., pp. 178-79.

94. Alfred Edersheim, *The Life and Times of Jesus the Messiah* (Grand Rapids, MI: Eerdmans, 1972), part 2, book 5, chapter 16, p. 621.

95. Ibid., p. 629.

96. Thomas Arnold, *Christian Life—Its Hopes, Its Fears and Its Close*, 6th ed. (London: T. Fellowes, 1859), p. 324, from McDowell, *More Than a Carpenter*, p. 96.

97. Michael Murphy, "The Two-Sided Game of Christian Faith" in John Warwick Montgomery ed., *Christianity for the Tough-Minded* (Minneapolis: Bethany House Publishers, 1973), p. 255, emphasis added.